CALL OF THE WILD

The Language of Cats and Other Felines

Alicia Z. Klepeis

Cavendish Square

New York

Published in 2017 by Cavendish Square Publishing, LLC
243 5th Avenue, Suite 136, New York, NY 10016

Copyright © 2017 by Cavendish Square Publishing, LLC

First Edition

CPSIA Compliance Information: Batch #CS16CSQ

All websites were available and accurate when this book was sent to press.

Library of Congress Cataloging-in-Publication Data

Names: Klepeis, Alicia Z.
Title: The language of cats and other felines / Alicia Z. Klepeis.
Description: New York : Cavendish Square, 2017. | Series: Call of the wild | Includes index.
Identifiers: ISBN 9781502617323 (pbk.) | ISBN 9781502617248 (library bound) | ISBN 9781502617125 (6 pack) | ISBN 9781502617187 (ebook)
Subjects: LCSH: Cats--Juvenile literature. | Cats--Behavior--Juvenile literature. | Animal communication--Juvenile literature.
Classification: LCC SF445.7 K54 2017 | DDC 636.8083--dc23

Editorial Director: David McNamara
Editor: Kelly Spence
Copy Editor: Rebecca Rohan
Art Director: Jeffrey Talbot
Designer: Joe Macri
Senior Production Manager: Karol Szymczuk
Photo Research: J8 Media

The photographs in this book are used by permission and through the courtesy of: AppStock/Shutterstock.com, cover; Vvvita/Shutterstock.com, 4; Volcko Mar/Shutterstock.com, 5; Akimasa Harada/Moment Open/Getty Images, 6; MogensTrolle/iStockphoto.com, 7; Zanna Holstova/Shutterstock.com, 8; Zanna Holstova/Shutterstock.com, 10; Ssgrafika/ iStockphoto.com, 11; Ger Bosma/Moment/Getty Images, 13; Noah Seelam/AFP/Getty Images, 14; Nolte Lourens/ Shutterstock.com, 15; travelstock.ca/Alamy Stock Photo, 16; Papilio/Alamy Stock Photo, 18; Robynrg/Shutterstock.com, 19; Micael Carlsson/Moment Open/Getty Images, 20; Tierfotoagentur/Alamy Stock Photo, 22; belizar/Shutterstock.com; 23; Elizabeth Livermore/Moment Open/Getty Images, 24; Erin "Dr. E" Nyren, "How Do Cats Purr?", Discovery Express Kids, LLC. discoveryexpresskids.com, Feb. 8, 2014., 26; Denis Farrell/AP Images, 27.

Printed in the United States of America

CONTENTS

Animal Communication

S aying hello. Waving to someone. Hugging your grandma. These are all ways that people communicate. Communication is an exchange of information. When individuals communicate, one person shares information with another who receives that information.

Animals communicate as well. But how? After all, animals do not speak a language like English or Spanish. Instead, animals have their own unique ways to share information. They can tell other creatures, including people, how they feel. There are lots of reasons that animals communicate.

4

Some are looking for a mate. Others send out warnings about danger. Animals also share information about what **territory** belongs to them and where to find food.

HOW CATS COMMUNICATE

Most animals, including cats, communicate using their five senses. Visual communication involves what a cat sees. Just like people, cats also use body language to show how they feel. A cat might blink at another cat it is curious about. Or it might hiss to warn another animal to stay away.

A housecat sits and relaxes by the window. Many people believe that a cat "smiles" and shows it is content by squinting its eyes.

THE SCIENCE BEHIND HOW CATS "TASTE" SMELLS

Cats have a special organ called a Jacobson's organ. This organ lets the cat "taste" a scent. Male cats use this organ to sniff out females during mating season. When a cat smells  something interesting, it collects the scent in its mouth, then uses its tongue to flick the scent up to the Jacobson's organ (in the roof of its mouth). The organ contains **ducts** leading to the cat's nose and mouth. All cats can use this organ anytime they think a smell needs to be examined further.

Cats also share information through scents. They release chemicals called **pheromones**. These chemicals carry messages to other animals.

Cats are best known for their sounds. A cat's meow can have many meanings. It could mean "I'm scared" or "I'm hungry." For **solitary** cats, like tigers, sounds can carry messages over long distances.

Touch is another way animals communicate. Cats rub up against each other to show affection. A mother cat nuzzles her newborn kittens.

A lion cub snuggles up to its older brother on Africa's Serengeti Plain.

Sitting under a table, a domestic cat cries for food. The cat makes this noise to tell its owner that it is hungry.

CHAPTER ONE

Housecat Conversations

ousecats are **domesticated** animals. They share information using their different senses. These include sight, sound, smell, and touch.

ALL SORTS OF SOUNDS

Housecats purr, growl, hiss, and meow. They might purr if they're happy, in pain, or very frightened. Some experts say purring is how cats express deep emotions. Others think purring is a way of saying, "Stay with me."

These cats look like they are kissing. But they are actually greeting each other by touching noses.

Cats also growl sometimes. They make these noises deep in their throats. Growling means "Stay away!" Cats hiss when defending themselves. A kitten might meow if it is lost or cold. Adult cats may meow if they are unhappy or need food. **Feral**, or wild, cats go about their daily lives without making much noise.

Touch is very important to cats. Cats that know each other may greet each other by touching noses. A cat's

SPECIES STATS

Housecats are meat eaters. On average, they are about 28 inches (71 centimeters) long, including their tails. Most cats weigh between 5 to 20 pounds (2.3 to 9 kilograms). The average housecat lives for fifteen years, although some live for more than twenty.

whiskers are sensitive to touch. They help a cat sense objects that they might not be able to see, like at night.

SCENT SIGNALS

Smell is an important way that cats exchange information. Cats have a much better sense of smell than people. Mother cats lick and **groom** their babies. This helps the kittens to identify their mother by her smell.

A cat sharpens its claws on a post. Other cats can see and smell these scratch marks.

Cats mark their territory in the wild. They use **urine** to tell other animals "This is my territory!" A cat's nose is so sensitive that it can tell what other cats have been in its neighborhood, when they were there, and for how long.

Cats also scratch to communicate. Scratching is both a visual and a scent-based way to send a message. Other cats can see the scratches on a tree or fence post. A cat's paws also contain scent **glands**. These glands leave behind smells that linger on the scratch marks.

11

As a tiger stretches, it sharpens its claws on the log. This leaves behind a scent that tells other animals the territory is occupied.

CHAPTER TWO

Tiger Talk

Tigers, like domestic cats, communicate in many different ways. They use body language to express their feelings. A tiger that feels threatened may arch its back. It does this to look bigger and more **intimidating** to an enemy. Tigers would rather scare enemies off with a warning than actually fight.

A tiger's tail contains a scent gland. The tiger sometimes rubs its tail on other tigers. This is a form of communication. It helps the tigers to recognize each other. Tail rubbing can also be part of a mating ritual between male and female tigers.

Smelling the scent left behind by its mother, a five-month-old white tiger cub follows in her footsteps.

A tiger also has scent glands in between its toes. These leave an individualized scent behind. This scent allows tiger cubs to follow in their mother's footsteps in the wild.

SIGHT AND SOUND

Tigers communicate with sounds. When tigers want to greet other tigers nearby, they sometimes **chuff**. Chuffing is a friendly noise. It sounds like a soft "brrr." It can only be heard at close range.

Mother tigers may moan at their babies. This is believed to be a gentle way of persuading them to do something. During mating season, male tigers may moan to relax the female tigers.

A hungry Siberian tiger warns others to stay away from its food.

Male tigers sometimes roar to find mates or to warn other male tigers to get out of their territory. A tiger's roar can be heard from nearly 2 miles (3.2 kilometers) away. Tigers may also snarl when they feel threatened. A tiger might snarl and hiss if it thinks another tiger wants to steal its food.

SPECIES STATS

Tigers are meat eaters. They are the biggest members of the cat family. A full-grown Bengal tiger can weigh anywhere from 240 to 500 pounds (109 to 227 kg). Their head-body length is 5 to 6 feet (1.5 to 1.8 meters) and their tails are often 2 to 3 feet (0.6 to 0.9 m) long. These endangered animals live between eight and ten years in the wild.

Most adult bobcats have a recognizable tuft of fur on top of each ear. Some researchers believe this extra fur helps the animals to hear better.

CHAPTER THREE

Bobcat Chat

Bobcats get their name from their short, bobbed tails. They are about twice the size of an average housecat. These wild animals use their sensitive whiskers to hunt. As the bobcat tries to capture its prey, the whiskers on its **muzzle** extend like a net in front of its face. This helps the bobcat figure out if its prey is moving—and where.

LONE RANGERS

Like many other cats, bobcats are mostly solitary. Bobcats use scent to mark their territories. They spray urine, **feces**, and other liquids from glands near their rear end. The marking warns other bobcats to stay away. Males and females usually only interact during mating season.

SOUNDING OFF

Bobcats are able to make many different sounds. But bobcats rarely **vocalize**. A bobcat's meow doesn't sound the same as a typical housecat's meow. When female bobcats are ready to mate, they **caterwaul**. This piercing sound is loud and intense. Bobcats often hiss and yowl when it's time to mate.

A mother bobcat nurses her cubs in the wild. Young bobcats usually nurse for the first two months of life.

Bobcat kittens will purr as they **nurse**. This is believed to mean they are content. If in distress, the kittens will make sad mewing sounds. Bobcat mothers may make a sudden growling sound to alert their kittens of danger. The kittens react to this alarm call by disappearing and

remaining still until they hear an "all clear" noise from their mother.

When bobcats fight, they growl, hiss, scream, and spit at each other until one bobcat retreats. This shows **submission** to a stronger bobcat.

SPECIES STATS

Bobcats are meat eaters. They typically prey on rabbits, birds, squirrels, mice, and other small animals. Their head-body length is 26 to 41 inches (66 to 104 cm), with another 4 to 7 inches (10 to 18 cm) for their tails. They weigh between 11 and 30 pounds (5 to 14 kg). Bobcats are found all over North America. They live in a wide variety of **habitats** including mountains, forests, and deserts. Bobcats live between ten and twelve years in the wild.

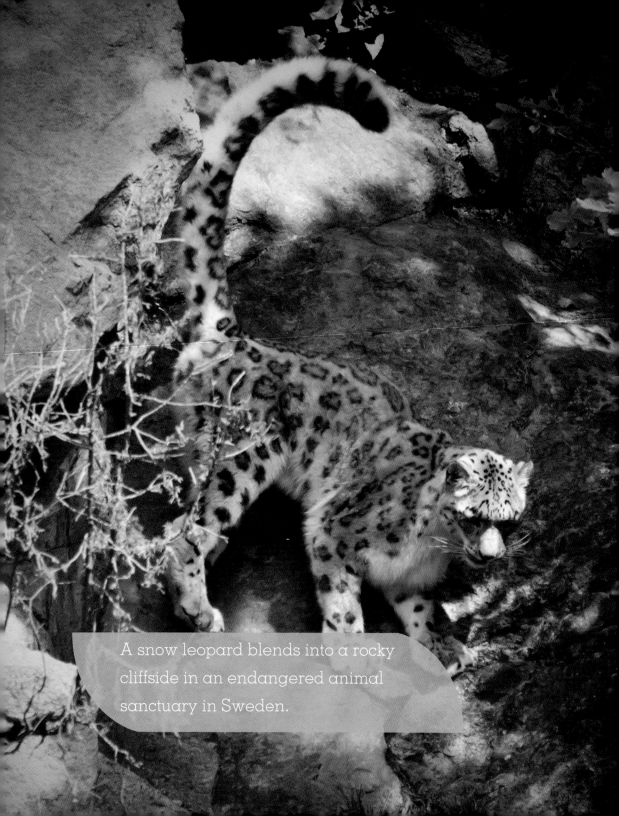

A snow leopard blends into a rocky cliffside in an endangered animal sanctuary in Sweden.

CHAPTER FOUR

Snow Leopard Speak

The snow leopard, nicknamed the "ghost of the mountain," is a hard animal to find. These cats roam the mountains of Central Asia. A single snow leopard may have a home range spanning hundreds of miles. But even these solitary creatures must communicate.

MESSAGE TRAILS

How do snow leopards get messages to other snow leopards? They leave markings in the snow or soil. Sometimes these big cats scrape the ground with their back legs, leaving V-shaped marks. Other snow leopards find these markings.

By rubbing its face on a tree, this snow leopard communicates with others through the scent and fur it leaves behind.

Snow leopards may also rub their cheeks on rocks and trees. This leaves some of their fur behind, as well as their scent.

The markers snow leopards leave behind serve many purposes. They identify the boundaries between leopards' home ranges. They also allow other snow leopards to find each other. For example, scent marking helps these animals find mates.

Besides scrapes, facial hair, and footprints, snow leopards often spray urine on rocks. Female snow leopards may also leave feces outside of their dens. Yuck! This creates a scent signal that is meant to make sure that no one bothers their babies.

SOUND SIGNALS

Snow leopards also make sounds to communicate. These sounds are used over short distances. These big cats purr, mew, growl, moan, chuff, and yowl. During mating season, female snow leopards make a continuous yowling sound to attract a male. Females also chuff more during this time of year.

Three snow leopard cubs crouch low in the grass.

SPECIES STATS

Snow leopards are meat eaters. Their head-to-body length can be up to 5 feet (1.5 m), with another 3 feet (1 m) of length in their tails. These big cats weigh between 60 to 120 pounds (27 to 54 kg). They live up to eighteen years in the wild. Snow leopards are an endangered species. There are estimated to be less than 7,500 snow leopards living in the wild.

A domestic cat rubs its head against its owner's head. This act makes the person smell familiar to the animal.

CHAPTER FIVE

A Conversation with Cats

Cats don't just communicate with other cats. They also communicate with people. Have you ever had a cat rub up against your leg? That cat was sending you a message. It was saying "hello."

WHISKER SIGNALS

A cat's whiskers show how it is feeling. If a cat's whiskers are bent forward, that means she is feeling friendly. If her whiskers are pulled back, stay away! Cats push their whiskers out of the way when they want to bite.

DECODING SOUNDS

Cats make lots of sounds to communicate with people. Adult cats can make somewhere between thirty and one hundred different sounds. Cats might purr while being petted. They don't purr when they are alone.

THE SCIENCE BEHIND A CAT'S PURR

Purring begins in a cat's vocal cords. Muscles in the walls of the cat's larynx (voice box) pull the vocal cords back and forth quickly, making them vibrate. This makes the purring sound. Nerves control the voice box muscles, setting the rhythm of the purr.

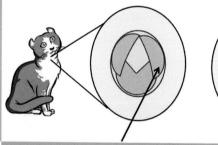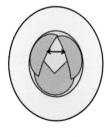

Cats have "false vocal cords" in their voice box. These vibrate when air rushes past them, creating a purring sound.

You might be surprised to find out that cats rarely meow at each other. Meows to people have many meanings. A cat might meow to ask for food or to go outside. Some owners can tell what their cats' different meows mean.

Even though cats are not trained in the same way as dogs, they are good communicators *if* you take the time to listen to what they are "saying."

IN THE FIELD

Kevin Richardson is a scientist who studies animal behavior. He works closely with lions and is nicknamed the "Lion Whisperer." He studies what makes individual lions happy or upset. Richardson's research methods are very unusual. He grooms, sleeps, plays, and even bathes with the lions he studies.

Glossary

caterwaul A piercing, high-pitched howling or wailing noise made by a cat.

chuff A soft snorting sound used by tigers and snow leopards as a greeting or to show excitement.

domesticated Describing an animal that has been tamed or trained by humans.

ducts Tubes or vessels for transporting something.

feces Bodily waste discharged from the bowels after food has been digested; poop.

feral In a wild state, especially after escaping from domestication or captivity.

glands Organs that release substances like sweat and saliva from the body.

groom To clean and keep up the appearance of.

habitats The places or kinds of places where plants and animals normally grow or live.

intimidating Frightening someone (or another animal), especially to make them do what one wants.

muzzle The part of an animal's face consisting of its mouth, nose, and chin.

nurse To feed a baby milk at the mother's breast.

pheromones Chemical substances that are produced and released into the environment by animals.

solitary Living or existing alone.

submission The action of giving in to a stronger individual.

territory An area belonging to one individual or group of individuals.

urine Waste material that is secreted by the kidneys, usually a yellowish liquid in mammals; pee.

vocalize To make sounds or words.

Find Out More

Books

Newman, Aline Alexander, and Gary Weitzman. *How to Speak Cat: A Guide to Decoding Cat Language.* Washington, DC: National Geographic Society, 2015.

Webster, Maureen. *Cat Speak: Revealing Answers to the Strangest Cat Behaviors.* Cats Rule! North Mankato, MN: Capstone Press, 2016.

Websites

National Geographic: Domestic Cat

animals.nationalgeographic.com/animals/mammals/domestic-cat

Read all about domestic cats.

SeaWorld: Tiger Communication

seaworld.org/Animal-Info/Animal-InfoBooks/Tiger/Communication

Learn more about how tigers communicate.

Index

About the Author

Alicia Z. Klepeis loves to research fun and out-of-the-ordinary topics that make nonfiction exciting for readers. Klepeis began her career at the National Geographic Society. She is the author of many kids' books, including *The World's Strangest Foods, Bizarre Things We've Called Medicine, Francisco's Kites,* and *From Pizza to Pisa.* She lives with her family in upstate New York.